Sweet Meditation

Copyright 2016 © Aleigha Israel
All rights reserved.
Written permission must be secured from the author
to use or reproduce any part of this book.

Printed in the USA by Createspace
www.createspace.com

Scripture taken from the HOLY BIBLE,
NEW KING JAMES VERSION, (unless otherwise
noted).

Printed in United States of America

Cover Design by Leisha Israel
www.digitaltractordesign.com

Interior Formatting

Sweet Meditation

By Aleigha Israel

Illustrated by
Daddy and Mama
Hannah, Claire,
Aidan, Owen,
Lucy, and Aleigha

*May my meditation be sweet to Him;
I will be glad in the Lord.*

PSALM 104:34

THIS BOOK IS DEDICATED TO
my sweet mother!
Words can't describe what a precious blessing you are in my life.
I don't want to imagine what my world would be like without you in it.
You make our family complete in every way!
I love you, Mama!

A NOTE TO MY READERS

Dear readers,

Upon putting together this book, I was once again confronted with the daunting words: "*A Note to My Readers.*"

I must say, writing this page was by far the hardest part in *Sweet Meditation*. Not writing the poems nor typing the poems nor getting together the adorable pictures was as difficult as putting all my thoughts together on one page. Because, as another author put it, "words are kind of my thing," and I do tend to be wordy sometimes, (believe it or not).

As I was reading Max Lucado's book, *A Gentle Thunder* the other day, I was enthralled with his analogy.

"A book should be a garden that fits in the hands.

Word-petals of color. Stems of strength. Roots of truth. Turn a page and turn the season. Read the sentence and enjoy the roses… of the many gardens you could visit, you've chosen to visit this one. I'm honored. I hope your stay is delightful…stay as long as you like. If you find a rose worth keeping, feel free to clip it. If you find a few worth sharing, please do.

And who knows? Adam heard God speak in a garden; maybe the same will happen to you."

He couldn't have said it better! My prayer, dear readers, is that you will be blessed and encouraged by these poems.

Thank you for taking the time to read this book.

May the Lord's blessings be upon you!

Aleigha C. Israel

Sweet Meditation

HE DID HIS BEST

The vastness of this earth
is quite hard to understand,
from the bright blue stretch of sky
to the tiny grains of sand.
From the miles of endless ocean,
to the setting of the sun,
the red rose sparkling with dew,
when the day has just begun.
The field with vibrant crops,
the eagle in the sky,
the gorgeous snow-capped mountains
stretching way up high.
The pretty falling leaves,
from the tree that's almost bare,
you can tell by just looking
it was made with so much care.
Our Father, the Creator
thought of everything He should,
I could never have thought of it all,
I just don't think I could.
From the North, the East, the South and the West,
you can tell by just looking,
the Lord did His best.

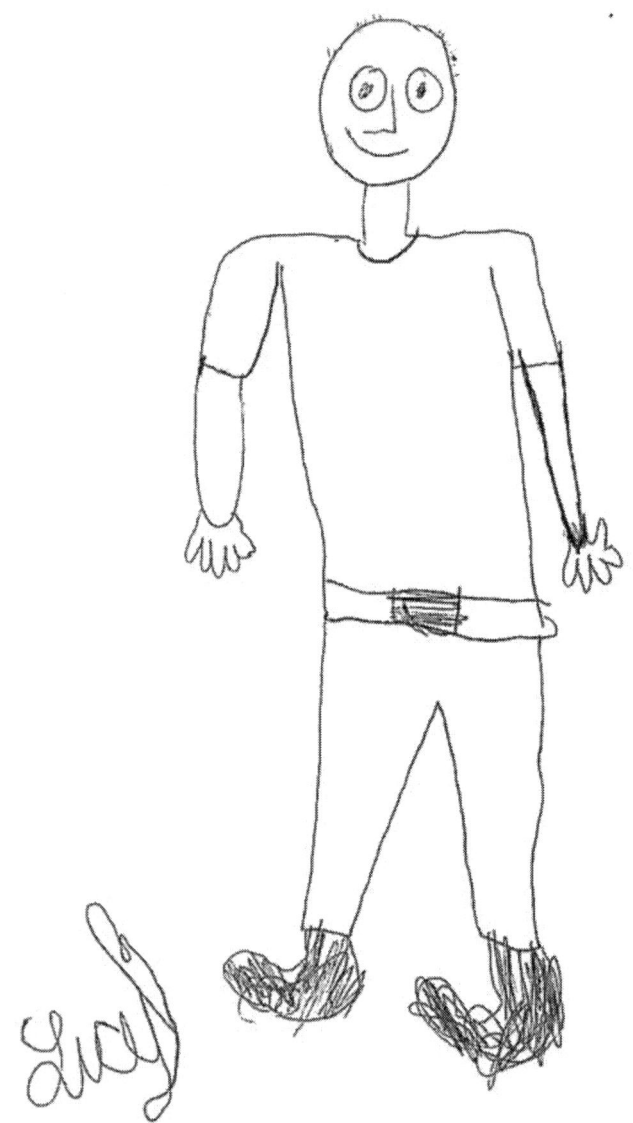

FATHERS

The father is the patriarch,
the leader of the home.
His protection stretching over the family
like some imaginary dome.
The father leads his family
to grow better every day,
spiritually and physically
in every little way.
Fathers correct and chasten,
for that's what they're supposed to do,
to help you grow up godly,
for they know what's best for you.
Fathers are wise with wisdom,
brought about from their fear of God.
Fathers are here for their children, however far that we
may trod.

MOTHERS

Mothers are a blessing
God sent from up above.
They have the endurance of a soldier,
the gentleness of a dove.
Mothers are here to make things better,
by a hug or word of cheer,
mothers are a comfort,
just knowing they are here.
Mothers are unselfish,
it's very plain to see,
for they strive to serve their family,
and they do it happily.
Mothers are here to give us
those little jewels about our day,
to teach us to love one another,
in every little way.
Such a blessing could only be sent,
by our Savior, up above,
so much tenderness and mercy,
joyfulness and love.
Mothers forgive us,
of every small and big transgression.
Yes, mothers are for sure,
a little glimpse of Heaven.

OUR ETERNAL HELPER

The feeling you get when a task is now done,
is the opposite feeling than when you'd begun.
It can be so overwhelming
to start a big task,
that we forget who will help us
if only we ask.
Jesus will be, more than happy I know,
to help you through your trials
for He's been watching you below.
So the next time you start a task
and need Jesus there,
just ask and listen
for you might just hear Him say;
I'm here when you need Me,
for I'm here to stay.

UNCONDITIONAL LOVE

As the Father loved me, I have also loved you;
Abide in My love, for My love is true.
If you keep my commandments, you will abide in My love,
just as I have in My Father's above.
These things I have spoken, that My joy may be in you,
that it may be full, strong, and true.
This is my commandment, that you love one another,
sister, brother, father and mother.
For I have loved you, and My Father loved Me,
so you should love others, it's plain to see.
Greater love hath no man than this,
than to lay down his life, for one of his friends.

OUR HOBBY FARM

A cow, some chickens, a horse or two,
is the start of a farm, I think; don't you?
A donkey adds a special touch,
then add some fowl, some quail and such.
You can't forget the pigs and sheep,
then add some goats who climb hills so steep.
You can build your farm, as big as you want,
so let's add some hogs who always grunt.
These hogs will be just for our meat,
I'm sure they'll be tasty, spicy and sweet.
You can't forget, a garden or two,
to grow the essentials, you'll need for you.
A big giant family and a house full of love,
and lots of help from our God up above.

Be anxious for nothing, but in everything by prayer and supplication, with thanksgiving, let your requests be made known to God; and the peace of God, which surpasses all understanding, will guard your hearts and minds through Christ Jesus.

PHILIPPIANS 4:6-7

THE PEACE OF GOD

If you had the peace of God, ruling in your life,
there'd be no room for an angry heart.
A hard and bitter countenance,
though it seems to be little, it plays a big part.
If you had the peace of God, ruling in your life,
you wouldn't have time for an angry tongue.
Constantly you would murmur,
"His will on earth, not mine be done."
If you had the peace of God, ruling in your life,
with love you would treat each other.
Love and kindness would be flowing,
to every sibling, father and mother.
If you had the peace of God, ruling in your life,
a gentle peace there would always be,
a peacefulness that never ceased too last,
whether on land or on the sea.

THE FABRIC STORE

Hang a left on joyful street
and there I'm sure you'll find,
"The Love and Mercy Fabric Store"
with colors of every kind.
There, they'll measure you just for size
the clothes will surely fit.
You will be greeted with a smile,
and then found a place to sit.
Once the measuring has ended
the best part is yet to come,
they know just what they're doing
it's way too fast for some!
One yard of salvation is definitely a must,
½ yard of mercy and ¼ yard of trust.
5 whole feet of kindness
are used to trim the dress.
20 bright pink buttons
are placed for righteousness.
They never forget love
it's added to the dress,
gentleness and praise
and then it's off to press!
Once in the pressing room
it's pressed with all they've got,
with perseverance and kindness
just how they were taught.
Then with an air of joyfulness

it's presented to the buyer,
what a beautiful dress
hung upon a simple wire.
When coming up to pay
you're then told, "it's free."
"But mind, it cost someone's
life upon a tree.
He died just for you
so that you may be free,
and live someday within His home
for eternity."

In every thing give thanks: for this is the will of God in Christ Jesus concerning you.
1 Thessalonians 5:18

THANK YOU

Lord, I thank You for the gift, You sent so long ago,
the best gift ever given, that I have ever known.
A precious newborn baby,
in a bed of straw at His mother's feet,
shepherds from the hills,
bowing at their Savior's feet.
I thank You for the sacrifice
You chose to give for me,
to hang that precious baby, someday upon a tree.
I thank You for Your plan, in making all things new,
in giving me a chance to do what's right to do.
I thank You, Lord, for making a path for me,
and giving me a map, the Bible I can read.
Thank You, Lord, for listening,
to my prayers both short and long,
and thank You for forgiving me
of all the wrong I've done.
I thank You for Your love,
which surrounds me every day,
pulling me out of sin, and showing me the way.

PICTURES

Pictures are like little boxes,
holding our memories tightly within,
just by looking at a picture
it can bring laughter or tears flowing from within.
Looking at pictures is a fun thing to sit down and do,
but take heed, for you never know what emotions
might start happening to you.
It might be a picture of a dog or a cat,
you realize is no longer here,
or of a child or parent, then memories draw near.
It could be a picture of creation,
which could remind you why you're here.
And strive to give God the glory,
the remainder of your time here.
You might see a picture of a place,
and many memories start to spin,
so many you have to stop and
think or they might jumble all within.
Yes, a picture is a box full of memories,
bright and true.
They are such very special things,
everyone should have a few.

A PRECIOUS BLESSING

The Bible is a blessing, in many ways it's true,
it's full of such wisdom and rules of things to do.
It teaches you the way,
when you're lost and off the path,
it's not hard to comprehend,
like some complicated math.
You could read it every day,
the rest of your whole life,
still learning things each day,
from love and mercy down to strife.
There's so much you can learn,
if you're willing and humble too,
you can never read too much,
it's just not possible to do!

Therefore be patient, brethren, until the coming of the Lord. See how the farmer waits for the precious fruit of the earth, waiting patiently for it until it receives the early and latter rain.

JAMES 5:7

PATIENCE

To be patient, friends,
isn't an easy task, as you can see,
it starts with a yearning,
and then with a quiet, humble plea.
But we must be patient,
that command came from the Lord,
for how else are we to live
with each other in one accord?
A farmer waits for his precious fruit;
he waits with a patient heart.
How long and wearisome it may be,
he is patient from the start.
Within this troubled world,
however hard that it may be,
we must be patient with each other
and live our life as God shall lead.
We must be patient friends,
and live in one accord.
We must continue to be patient,
until the coming of our Lord.

Anger does a man more hurt than that which made him angry.
CHARLES SPURGEON

ANGER

Anger is like poison,
with its deadly darts of woe,
shooting at its victims
from towers of death below.
Anger only shatters
but the love which work has done,
causing you to live in the life
of the dreary one.
Anger is like death,
a slow death of the heart,
causing you to drift,
farther and farther apart.
First you lose respect,
respect that once was yearned.
Then love is lost in anger,
the love which you had earned.
Your friend is turned to foe,
one grasp of life but to let go;
all by one simple word,
but such power it does hold.
The power of anger,
its truth to be told.
I mustn't go on to tell,
how the power of anger may,
grasp you with its hold and
whittle you away.

But the love and forgiveness of Christ,
that was put into our heart,
can win the war against the anger
if we strive to do our part.
Loving God and loving others,
treating family as a friend,
can help to be the start
that puts anger to an end.
A soft word helps to turn away,
what otherwise would be wrath,
praying for more strength
to cross hurdles in our path.
We must pray and ask God's mercy
on our anger in every way,
that the Lord may take away the anger
and cause us to walk worthy, day by day.

Rejoice in the Lord always. Again I will say, rejoice!

PHILIPPIANS 4:4

REJOICE

If your day seems all jumbled and your life is a mess,
your time seems to disappear, leaving you pressed.
And your moments of silence are all dark and drear,
and the urge to cry is ever so near.
Then it may be time to tidy something,
not a room or a house, but your ever present being.
Are you putting Jesus first in every small task?
Is your love for each other, under a mask?
Are you putting yourself last, in every small thing? If
you're doing these things,
then you should have the urge to sing!
For by following these steps it helps to bring us joy,
for true joy can't be fulfilled by a thing or a toy.
So the next time you are anxious, troubled or sad,
don't get discouraged and downright mad.
But remember these words from the Bible just a bit;
"...this is the day the Lord has made;
let us rejoice and be glad in it!"

ONE SPOTLESS LAMB

A quiet, peaceful lamb,
its color as white as snow,
it's interesting to hear how
they were talked of long ago.
An atonement for their sins,
these little lambs were slain,
given as a sacrifice, perfect, small and plain.
But not one of these small lambs
could do what one did that sunny day,
as He took up all our sins
and washed them clean away.
If it wasn't for that Lamb,
perfect, spotless, white as snow;
it's hard to think of that place
we would be sure to have to go.
But He took the punishment we deserved
as He died upon a tree,
so that we could live with Him forever, in eternity.

CANDY

Candy's fun to look at,
it's more enjoyable though to eat,
the sweet sugary goodness is definitely a treat.
There's lots of varieties of candy,
shapes and sizes too.
As you walk into a candy shop,
it's staring back at you.
There's truffles and gummy bears, lollipops too,
so many molds of chocolate, "Look!
That one is shaped like a kangaroo!"
It's amazing to taste how candy can
pack such a flavor,
as every little bit you buy,
you try so very hard to savor.

the fruit of the Spirit is...

gentleness, patience, Joy, Love, peace, kindness, self control, goodness, faithfulness

mama

"...THE FRUIT OF THE SPIRIT IS *LOVE, JOY, PEACE...*"

Peace and mercy, patience and love,
are all sweet gifts that come from above.
But hatred, strife and envy too,
are things that will constantly eat at you.
You can try to be good on your own, you can try,
if you were told you will succeed,
there's never been a bigger lie.
There's no one that is good, no not one,
only one person passed that test,
sent from His Father and called His Son.
A baby full of love, as perfect as can be,
was sent to be the sacrifice,
a sacrifice for you and me.
Faithfulness and gentleness and self-control,
are gifts we can strive to use and gladly play its role.
But discontentment and anger, discord, yes all three,
are things to put to death if we're to live peaceably.

MAN'S COMPANION

Dogs are man's companion,
They've been here from the start.
Those honest truthful eyes,
that go right to your heart.
The soft patter of paws,
that downcast look of shame,
when they've broken all your laws.
That friendly bark of welcome,
that greets you when you're home.
Your loyal furry friend knows not far to roam.
Our constant companions, never to leave our side.
In our homes, with trust they abide.
Some dogs are the eyes, that help the blind to see.
Dogs are pretty smart, or though it seems to me.
I think the Lord knew what He was doing
when He made our little friend,
that loyal ball of fur, by our side until the end.

Death is no punishment to the believer; it is the gate of endless joy.

CHARLES SPURGEON

MEMORIES UNBROKEN

Our lives are so short, with such little time,
to tell those that we love, the heart of this rhyme.
When our loved one's eyes
are closed peacefully in death,
there's so much we meant to say,
but we just can't go back.
When their last breath is drawn,
their last words now spoken,
you think back through your life,
memories unbroken.
How many times you forgot to say, "I love you,"
as you closed your eyes upon the day.
How many times a harsh word
you threw angrily their way.
How many times you argued upon trivial things;
they all seem so unimportant,
now that your thoughts have taken wings.
But your thoughts now shift
to the time you *did* have together.
Sweet precious memories,
nothing can snatch them away,
not the strongest storm in the weather.
The night that you met,
and knew that "he was the one."
When you set the date for the wedding,
so many plans to be done!

That very precious memory,
as husband and wife, you were joined as one;
by far one of the best things you've ever done.
The day when you told him, he was going to be a dad.
A fireworks of emotion, but none of them sad.
Birthdays and anniversaries,
special parties pass you by,
adding one more happy memory
to your collection by and by.
Those peaceful mornings in church,
sitting by the one you love;
as you clasp his hand tightly,
your heart is full of thanks to God above.
Now you're back to the moment,
but you refuse to say good-bye.
With a final kiss you murmur; "not forever, my love,
for you'll be waiting for me on high."

REFLECTION

The more and more I look into the mirror,
the more and more I see,
a face that's aging every passing day,
staring back at me.
The more and more I look upon the earth,
cursed from Adam's fall.
I marvel at how the world will stop turning,
at a single trumpet's call.
The more and more I look into God's word,
those nuggets of wisdom so right and true,
I thank the dear Lord for saving my soul,
and giving me eyes anew.
The more and more I grow older
and someday draw my last fleeting breath,
I know with assurance where my soul will find rest
When I at last, close my eyes in death.

TRAVELING THE WAY

A loving caring Savior, a joy from day to day,
a quiet peace that He, can bathe our tears away.
A time of rest while shadowed,
in the palm of His loving hand,
the king our Lord and Savior,
who loves us more than every ocean,
than every tiny grain of sand.
The king upon a throne,
in a mansion with streets of gold,
walls lined with precious gems,
it's a sight so beautiful to behold.
The privilege to bow before those nail pierced feet,
the thought that our sin brought them about,
is anything but sweet.
But knowing that in His heart,
He has forgiven us this day,
hand in hand with our Savior,
we'll finish traveling the way.

BOOKS

Books can take you to places,
you've never dreamed of ever going.
Like a land of candy,
where a chocolate stream never ceases flowing.
Or a land of kings and queens,
all made of pretzel rods,
or a family of peas, living in bright green pods.
Or they can take you to places,
of past history so very true.
In a place where people were killed for their beliefs,
when they did what's right to do.
You can read of places, past and present too,
and about the future,
things they say someday they'll do.
Books can take you to worlds,
and places and spots and things,
so grab yourself a book, and sit by a flowing stream.
Yes, books can take you places,
you've never dreamed you'd ever be,
full of adventure,
life and faraway places and full of history.

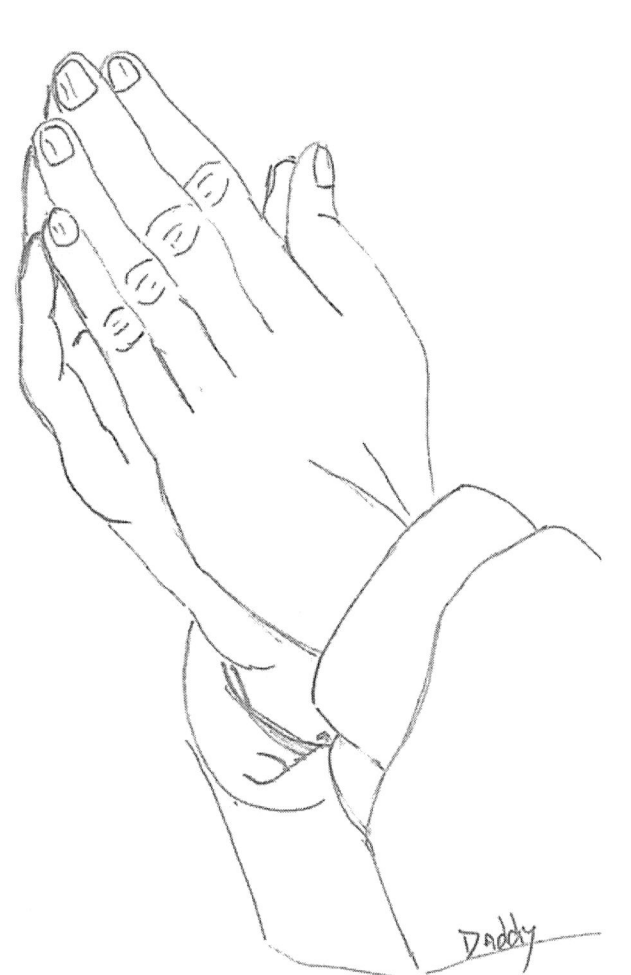

JUST TRUST AND PRAY

Anxiety never helped to calm a storm or raging sea.
It never helped to calm the nerves of you and me.
It never helped us with that test,
we knew we couldn't fail;
It only caused us to fail that test,
we should have then prevailed.
It caused Jesus' disciples
to trust not within His power.
When they should have trusted fully,
as if in the lightest shower.
"Be anxious for nothing"
the Bible clearly states, but in prayer,
may your requests be made known
to the Lord in every way.
You see, if we trust and not let anxiety rule our way,
we will find that we live more peaceably
in our life from day to day.

I know that nothing is better for them than to rejoice, and to do good in their lives, and also that every man should eat and drink and enjoy the good of all his labor—it is the gift of God.

ECCLESIASTES 3:12-13

JUST STOP A MINUTE

There once lived a lady who did things so fast,
that all of life's joys just whizzed her right past.
She didn't stop to watch the sunrise at morn,
she didn't have time for the woman sad and forlorn.
She never did pause to play with baby so sweet,
oh, she didn't have time to wash that traveler's feet.
Life passed all too quickly for that lady, yes it's true,
that she didn't think of being joyful,
though it's the right thing to do.
Each task was surrounded with the motive as before,
"just get this task done,
now on to mopping that floor!"
But oh, if that woman would have just
paused with her day, she would have seen
that life's more special that way.
For if we love one another and are joyful in all we do,
it makes tasks more enjoyable and others happy too.

*For to me, to live is Christ,
and to die is gain.*
PHILIPPIANS 1:21

THE HIGHEST HONOR

To give up your life for Christ
is something few would choose to do,
to share the blessed story,
even when it becomes dangerous to pursue.
They care not of themselves
but others and their souls lost to their god,
not even when thinking twice that it could end with
their body beneath the sod.
For to die for Christ would be such an honor
and they're excited to share His story,
even if it means death on their behalf,
to them they deem it glory.
There are but few who would give their life for sharing
a story about God's love.
But as they're martyred for their faith,
they'll soon be smiling up above.

A VISIT TO OAKLENBROOKE FARM
(A CHILDREN'S STORY)

Today we're going to Oaklenbrooke Farm,
I can hardly stand the wait.
Let's hurry and get ready, it wouldn't do to be late.
So don your mittens, your hat, scarf and coat,
we'll go visit the pigs, cows, sheep and a goat.
For you see all these animals were made
with such care, are you ready?
Set, go! I'll beat you there!
Do you see that silly donkey
with his funny sounding bray?
That goat looks so smart,
if he could talk, what would he say?
Look at that messy pig all covered in dirt.
Oh no! Watch out!
He's slung some on your shirt!
Let's head on over to the giant red barn,
away from mud-slinging pigs,
(though I doubt he meant harm)
Do you smell that hay? It's so fresh and sweet,
but let's stop for a break, I'm ready to eat.
Did you know that pigs have 44 teeth?
Or that cows have 4 stomachs, now isn't that neat?
I'm done with my lunch, are you finished with yours?
Let's see if the farmer will let us help with the chores.
After placing fresh hay in the hen's nesting box,
let's head on over to the pond, by the old boat dock.

Do you see that mother duck
with her ducklings in a row?
That pony's headed straight for us!
Whoa, pony whoa!
Phew, we're okay, but boy that was close!
If we hadn't moved fast
he would have stepped on our toes!
Oh, look at the sun,
it's time to start back.
If we head on home now,
we can walk the old train track.
Now wasn't today fun?
What was *your* favorite part?
I still think that goat looked so very smart.
Well, we're back now, and I must say thanks,
for coming, as it wouldn't have been
half so much fun alone....
And I know one thing for sure,
there's no place like home.

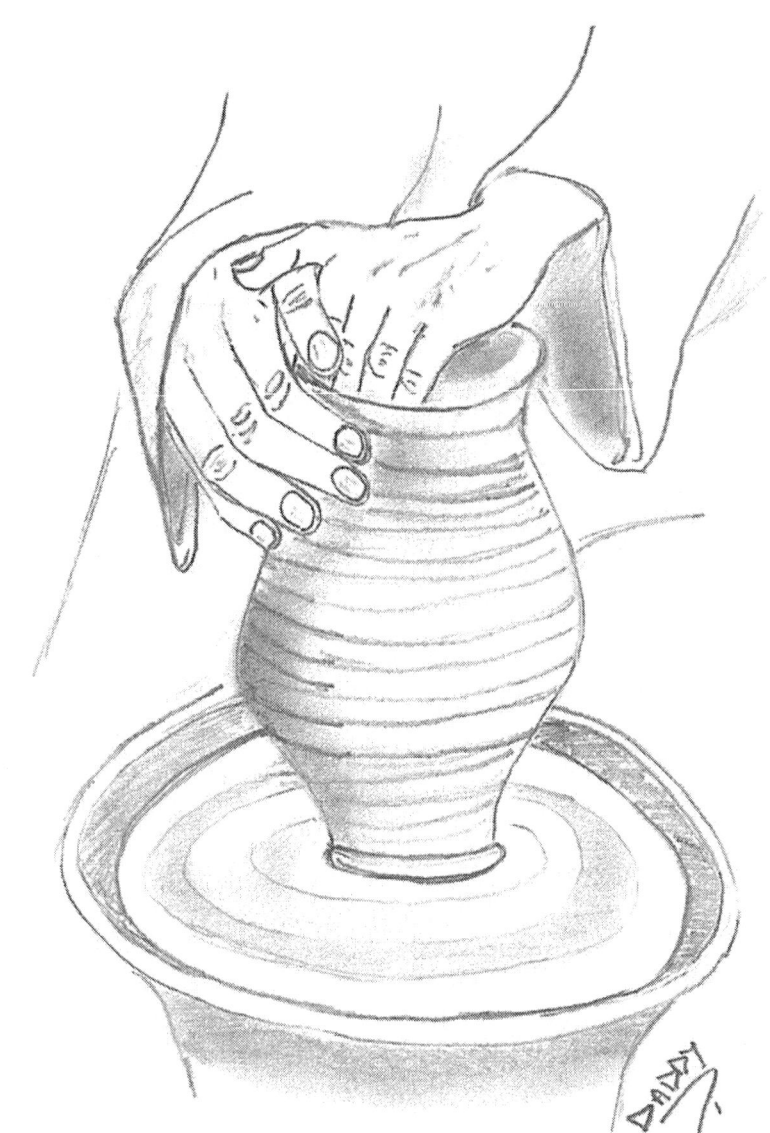

WE ARE HIS

He'll never leave us nor forsake us,
He's the potter, we're the clay.
He hung the moon to light the night
and made the sun to rule the day.
He sent His Son to take our sin,
a blessed peace upon our soul.
To break us down in humbleness
and with His love He makes us whole.
He provides for every need,
and calls us as His own.
What a blessedness it is to us,
what His precious life atoned.
What a blissful thought it is to know you're protected
where e're you go,
when you wake in the morning,
or when your eyes close in sleep.
With a precious hand you are shadowed,
your life, His to keep.

Thank you so much for taking a break with me and reading my poetry!

In gratitude, here is the first chapter of my first novel, A Higher Ransom. I hope you enjoy it!

Laus Deo!

Aleigha C. Israel

Will Anna stand strong and not waver in her faith? Or will she crumble under the rule of the heartless king?

A Higher Ransom

a novel by

ALEIGHA C. ISRAEL

One

Anna Haddington took a deep breath of the salty air. This was her stop, her last stop to her new destination, which she still could not call home. *Not yet*, she told herself stubbornly.

Anna brushed aside her dark brown hair as the wind whipped it about her face.

Children ran about the ship's deck in a lively game of tag, and the happiness could almost be felt. They had finally arrived and docked safely at the coast of Carpathia. She walked back over to the stern of the ship. Her gaze drifted absently out at the sea, not focusing on the scenery but trying to sort through all that had happened in the past few months.

It was startling how much could happen in such a short time. Only three weeks before, she had lived in a small cottage in France with her dear father and four precious siblings. The death of their mother had caused much grief to them all, but they had somehow managed to flow gently back into their daily routine of life and had even found things to laugh about again.

But that was almost a year ago, shortly after Isaiah was born. So much had happened since then. The past few weeks had gone by so rapidly, she hadn't even had time to think it all through properly until now.

Her father had been weak and ill for many months, and she should have suspected it, but maybe she was too naïve to understand or perhaps she just didn't allow herself.

Anna's chin trembled with emotion as she thought of her father. He was so loving and gentle and always smiling. Up until the days that sickness overtook him, he had been a very hard worker. As a farmer, there were many chores that needed his attention.

Her father loved the Lord with all he had. She knew without a doubt that he was in heaven right now, with her mother, rejoicing before the feet of their Savior.

They had never been poor, though they had lived a very humble life, not wasting money on frivolous things. Because their father was unable to work those last few months, their supply of money had slowly ran out. She had offered to take a job in town, but he wouldn't allow it.

"The Lord will provide, Anna dear. He always has and He always will."

She wished she had his faith.

Tears fell as she thought of her brothers and sisters she had left behind. Her brother Caleb had just turned ten. She remembered how, even at such a young age, he had such a fire for Christ. He would share God's love with everyone he met. He, especially, had been trying to witness to a young girl in a Muslim family. The young girl's name was Amira. Anna knew that Caleb would never stop witnessing to her and sharing God's love.

She thought of her sisters Margret and Julianna. They had made her parting much harder than she would have chosen. Their sweet personalities and the fun times they had shared would never be forgotten. And the baby of the family was Isaiah. His smile and bubbly personality had been a joy to them all.

After both parents' deaths, the children had been separated and split between two families within the church.

At eighteen years of age, Anna could have been a lot of help to many families, but the Lord seemed to have had other plans. Soon after her father's death, she received a letter from her aunt in Carpathia. After hearing of her brother's death, Jane wanted to help in any way she possibly could. She offered Anna a place to stay within her home and sent money for passage to come and live with her, along with a few coins for extra expenses. At any other time and place, Anna would have said no at once, but now, after everything that had happened, she was inclined to say yes, though she knew that she could not possibly answer such an important letter without consulting her Heavenly Father. After much prayer and consideration, she replied, letting her aunt know when to expect her. She had never been on a ship before and the preparations took her a few days. She almost changed her mind right before leaving, but a part inside of her told her that this was the right decision.

Now she was gone, and there was no turning back. She would go to live with her aunt and try to start a new life, a life, she hoped, that would make her parents proud.

Things must turn out better from here, right? Anna asked herself. *I had felt peace about this decision, and God knew best, didn't He?*

She chided herself for even considering to doubt God's guidance and direction, and decided that from now on she would try her best not to doubt God and His plans. He knew best for her life and she would fully trust Him. Whatever happened, she knew she was under His sovereign care and mercy.

As she made her way towards the front of the ship, she walked with a new reassurance, a reassurance that everything was going to be fine. A quiet peace settled over Anna as she remembered a verse in Romans:

> *"And we know that all things work together for good to them that love God, to them who are the called according to His purpose."*

Anna walked down the ship's ramp, scanning the crowd of people for her aunt.

"Watch your step!" warned a pleasant-faced man as he extended his hand.

"Merci, sir." Anna gave him a quiet smile.

"My pleasure, Miss," he replied, with a touch of his hat.

Anna looked around the dock, not exactly sure as to what or whom she was looking for. *Did Aunty say she would be meeting me here?* Anna tried hard to remember. *Maybe she was going to send someone.*

She walked toward a bench that looked quite welcoming and decided to stay there until her aunt's arrival. She positioned her carpet bag beside her and smiled at a little girl passing by. The girl had to be at least three, Anna guessed.

She reminded Anna of her own sister, Margret, who was around the same age. She was a joyful little girl with a fun personality.

The little girl smiled back at Anna and happily waved her tiny hand. But in the midst of looking up, the child tripped. She tried to catch herself, but to no avail. Anna quickly left her seat in hopes to catch her, but it was too late. The little girl fell to the ground and let out a piercing wail.

Anna bent down and picked up the child, holding her close and offering words of comfort. She brushed the dirt off the light blue dress and took off the little girl's now disheveled cream-colored bonnet. She took the tiny hands in hers and patted them gently.

"You'll be all right." Anna hoped her tone was soothing. "My name is Anna. What is yours?"

"Mary," the child spoke softly, drying her tears. "I'm fwee," Mary responded, holding up three tiny fingers to accompany her statement.

"Oh," Anna exclaimed, in mock astonishment, "you are almost a lady!"

Mary smiled a crooked grin, and clapped her hands. "Mama!" she crooned happily as a young woman in a soft pink dress came walking towards them. The dress was made of silk, as far as Anna could tell, and was adorned with several bows and yards of delicate lace.

"Mary!" the lady exclaimed. "My dear child, you gave Mama quite a scare!"

Anna stood up swiftly, the child still in her arms.

"I fell, Mama, see?" Mary said, sticking out her hands for her mother to inspect.

"So you did, you poor dear!" she replied, kissing her daughter's fingers.

"I couldn't find her anywhere! I was scared half to death," the lady said, turning to Anna. "And I've been so frantic, I misplaced the tickets and then I was sure we had lost a piece of luggage, and when I turned around, Mary was gone!"

Anna looked at the lady and nodded sympathetically.

"Oh, I seem to have misplaced more than just my tickets, where are my manners?" she stammered. "I'm Linda Hollingwood, and I see you have already met my Mary."

"And I'm Anna. I'm very pleased to meet you," Anna answered genuinely. "If there is anything that I can help you with, please don't hesitate to ask."

"Actually," Linda answered, "since you two seem to have bonded so well already, would you mind watching her for a few more minutes just until I get all of our things settled?"

"No, not at all, I would be delighted!"

"Good! I will be back soon."

Linda turned around and walked briskly back toward the ticket station.

Anna sat back down on the rustic bench and placed the child gently upon her lap.

"I goin' to ride on a big boat!" Mary exclaimed happily, settling herself in Anna's lap.

"That sounds exciting! Do you like to sing?" Anna inquired, changing the subject completely.

"Sing?" Mary mimicked, tilting her head to one side.

Anna laughed. "Yes, sing. A song or hymn, whichever is your favorite. Don't you sing songs in church?"

"Church!" Mary clapped her hands happily. "I like church!"

"I do, too," Anna agreed. "What songs do you sing in church?"

"Faiwist Jesus!" the child replied.

"Can you sing it for me?"

Mary nodded her head vigorously. With her sweet childish voice, she began to sing the first stanza of Fairest Lord Jesus.

"Faiwist Lord Jesus, ruler ub all nature,
O Thou ub God and man the Son,

*Vee will I cherish, Vee will I honor,
Thou, my soul's glory, joy and cwown."*

"That was lovely!" Anna told Mary in surprise. "You must have a very good memory to recall so many words! Did your mama help you learn them?" At the mention of the child's mother, Anna knew she had made a mistake. Mary's face instantly filled with alarm as she looked around with a troubled face.

"Mama?" Her eyes filled with tears. "Mama left me!"

"No, no, little one! She only left for a few minutes and she will be back soon." Anna tried to assure her.

But Mary was not convinced. She started to cry louder and louder until Anna was unsure of what to do. She looked around, praying that she would see the child's mother. Just when Anna thought she would be unable to handle the child's cries any longer, a black and white dog came wandering through the crowd. Anna pointed out the dog to Mary.

"Puppy!" Mary exclaimed, reaching out for the dog, who instantly licked the face of his newfound friend.

Anna sighed in relief and sat back watching Mary carefully. Mary dried her tears and played with the dog until it slowly wandered away.

"Puppy's gone," she murmured sadly.

Afraid that she may start crying again, Anna quickly tried to think of something that would divert Mary's attention. She softly began to sing one of her father's favorite songs:

> "There is a land of pure delight,
> Where saints' immortal reign;
> Infinite day excludes the night,
> And pleasures banish pain.
>
> There everlasting spring abides,
> And never-with'ring flow'rs;
> Death, like a narrow sea, divides
> This heav'nly land from ours.
>
> Sweet fields beyond the swelling flood
> Stand dressed in living green;
> So to the Jews old Canaan stood,
> While Jordan rolled between."

Anna looked down at Mary who was watching her with undivided attention. Several heads turned at the sound of Anna's singing. Mary let out a tired yawn and rested her little head against Anna's shoulder. Anna smiled at the child and continued singing in her clear soprano voice.

"But tim'rous mortals start and shrink
*   To cross this narrow sea;*
And linger, shiv'ring, on the brink,
*   And fear to launch away.*

O could we make our doubts remove,
*   Those gloomy doubts that rise,*
And see the Canaan that we love
*   With unbeclouded eyes;*

Could we but climb where Moses stood,
*   And view the landscape o'er,*
Not Jordan's stream, nor death's cold flood,
*   Should fright us from the shore.*

Mary's gentle breathing told Anna that she had fallen asleep. And it was good timing, for soon thereafter Mary's mother came out through the crowd to retrieve her daughter.

"Oh," Linda spoke softly. "Thank you so very much. You can't imagine how much of a blessing this has been to me!"

She bent down and gently picked up her sleeping daughter.

"It was my pleasure, ma'am," Anna replied.

She watched as they disappeared through the crowd. Anna looked around. The sun had started its daily descent down the mountain and a slight chill was coming with it. She picked up her luggage and decided to step into the small building that served as both a waiting room and ticket office. Once inside, she felt a drastic change. It was quiet indoors, and only then did she realize how loud it had been outside.

She sat down in a chair close to the window and told herself not to worry. *Aunty will be here soon.*

But, deep down, she felt a twinge of anxiety. *I have to trust!*

But it was so hard. Her thoughts flew quickly to a verse in John.

> "Peace I leave with you: My peace I give unto you: not as the world giveth, give I unto you. Let not your heart be troubled, neither let it be afraid."

She glanced out the window. People were coming and going, picking up and dropping off their loved ones. Everywhere she looked there were horses, wagons and buggies. A family stood off to the side offering tearful goodbyes to a young lady whom Anna assumed was their daughter. The young lady gently embraced a small child who had flung its arms around her neck. She watched as the father and mother embraced the young lady, and it was then that she realized how much she missed the embrace of her own dear parents. She also knew how hard it was to leave behind a loved one, not knowing if you would ever even see them again.

"Excuse me, Miss," an older gentleman spoke, interrupting Anna's thoughts. He was dressed in a black suit with silver buttons that traveled its entire length. He was tall, with greyish hair and a beard that seemed to add severity to his posture. At first appearance, he was formal and stern, but upon second glance, he looked as if he *could* laugh if the occasion arose.

"Are you waiting for someone?" he inquired, his tone was kind.

"Yes, sir, I am waiting for my aunt." Anna spoke in the sweetest voice she could muster.

"Did she say she would be meeting you here?"

"I am not quite certain, sir, though I do remember her saying something along those lines. But our train was delayed in Hingham for almost a week before our departure here, so she may not have known the exact date of my arrival."

"I see," the man said, not taking his eyes off of her. "And who might you be?" he asked.

"Oh, I'm Anna Haddington," Anna replied, her words holding a slight apologetic tone for not introducing herself sooner.

He shook Anna's hand and gave her a slight bow.

"I'm pleased to make your acquaintance, Miss Haddington," he said, his mustache twitching as if trying hard not to smile. "And who is your aunt?"

"Jane Willowbee," Anna replied.

All of the color drained from the gentleman's face as the words escaped Anna's lips.

"Jane who?" he choked, his voice sounding strained and forced.

"Willowbee," Anna replied. "Jane Willowbee."

A lady, sitting only a few feet away from Anna, gasped. Another lady in the corner sighed heavily and said, "oh, the poor thing."

Anna observed the gentleman in confusion. "What is it?" she gasped, her voice breaking. Anna's face turned ashen white as she awaited the gentleman's response. She felt unable to breath as her heart caught in her throat.

"I'm sorry to have to be the one to tell you this ma'am," he spoke quietly, "but your aunt is dead."

A Higher Ransom is available for purchase at www.thepenofthewriter.weebly.com

The HSW Method

Hear It, See It, And Write It!

Did you know that when you memorize a song, it makes the words really hard to forget?

We have gone once a month for several years to an assisted living home, playing music and singing for the residents. You would be surprised at how many of those sweet residents still remember the words and tunes to so many of the songs that we sing.

Hearing the scriptures put to music is a key ingredient to easy memorizing.

So, upon that note, (no pun intended) let's get started!

Hear It:

Put music to the scriptures.

Take the verses that you would like to memorize and try putting music to them. It can be music from a song that you like or a completely made-up tune. It also helps if you split the verse into sections. I have put an example below:

I Corinthians 13:4
- Love suffers long and is kind
- Love does not envy
- Love does not parade itself
- Is not puffed up

Memorize each section of the verse and then add on another section. Before you know it you will have the entire verse memorized!

See It:

Take your verse and read it. Over and over and over again. Read it using a strong inflection upon a different word each time. Put an exaggerated inflection on each bold word below:

- **Love** suffers long and is kind, love does not envy, love does not parade itself, is not puffed up.

- Love **suffers** long and is kind, love does not envy, love does not parade itself, is not puffed up.

- Love suffers **long** and is kind, love does not envy, love does not parade itself, is not puffed up.

- Love suffers long **and** is kind, love does not envy, love does not parade itself, is not puffed up.

Keep doing that until all the words have been used up. You will be amazed at how different it sounds, too! You might even learn something new by reading it that way. Do that a few times until you are ready to move on.

Write It:

Get a piece of paper and copy your verse. Copy it at least five times. After that you should be able to write it almost without looking.

Well, that's all, folks!
Remember, don't get discouraged, and have fun! Memorizing God's word is not only a fun thing to do, but it is also commanded:

"This Book of the Law shall not depart from your mouth, but you shall meditate in it day and night, that you may observe to do according to all that is written in it. For then you will make your way prosperous, and then you will have good success."
Joshua 1:8

"Let the word of Christ dwell in you richly in all wisdom, teaching and admonishing one another in psalms and hymns and spiritual songs, singing with grace in your hearts to the Lord."

Colossians 3:16

"I have not departed from the commandment of His lips; I have treasured the words of His mouth more than my necessary food."

Job 23:12

Memorize as many scriptures as you can. Believe me, they will soon come in handy!

Notes:

- It's important to memorize only one verse at a time. Once you have it down, then add another verse, saying both verse one and verse two one after the other.

- You may find it necessary to use only one part (Hear It, See It, or Write It) to memorize a scripture. For example, I can put a tune to the scripture and read it a few times, without having to write it down. Just play with it and see what works best for you.

- Remember, have fun and take joy in hiding God's Word in your heart!

Manufactured by Amazon.ca
Bolton, ON